Groaning and Singing

☙

Judy Kronenfeld

Judy Kronenfeld

FUTURECYCLE PRESS
www.futurecycle.org

Cover artwork by Lavina Blossom; author photo by Alexis Rhone Fancher; cover and interior design by Diane Kistner; Adobe Garamond Pro text and Caliban titling

Library of Congress Control Number: 2021951190

Copyright © 2022 Judy Kronenfeld
All Rights Reserved

Published by FutureCycle Press
Athens, Georgia, USA

ISBN 978-1-952593-22-2

Contents

I

Musical Surprise..7
A Familiar Train of Religious Observances...................................8
Inner Zest...10
Paid Work..12
My Mother, the Milkmaid, and Myself..14
Dream Displacements..16
Stemma...18
This Country...19
Selling...21
Tiny Apartment Early Girlhood Recall.......................................22
On the Roof..23
Saving the Dead...24

II

Late..29
Short Dream of Old Terror..30
Brief Drift...31
Non-Teaching Day..32
Wish...33
Ageism..34
Chronic This and That...36
Blurted Psalm, Night before Surgery..37
Coming Up from Under, after Surgery for Multiple Fractures...........38
Couple Observed..39
4 A.M., Suddenly Awake...40
Banana Bread Bake...41
Even Song..42

III

Astonished Shoes..45
The Natural World..46
How It Is, in Time...47
Scare-Crone..48
Now..50
Definitional..51
Gold..52
My 8-Year-Old Granddaughter Discovers
    the Arbitrariness of the Sign..53

IV

Letter to the Ministry of Loneliness..57
City...58
The Room..59
Not Getting the Mail...60
Distraction..61
Charm..62

V

Girl Brushing Her Hair in a Window..65
Here, We Are Gathered..66
Going Downhill...67
The Unasked Question..69
Voted America's Best Cemetery...70
Care..71
Physical..72
Catch and Release..73
The Comfort of Design..74

VI

Number and Weight...77
The Evening News...78
All-Purpose Elegy...79
The Watchers...80
Unfinished Painting...81
Stillness..82
Terrestrial...83

1

Musical Surprise

All through the klezmer concert
at the synagogue, all through the wailing, laughing,
talk-back violin, the clarinet cavorting
and kazatski-ing, and climbing up to cry
from the rooftops, the cymbals shushing and tsk-ing,
the sax keening and weeping its ecstasy
of prayer, my dead father and mother sit down beside me,
and my unmet father's sister who never fled
Germany, and my mother's parents
who died before I was born, and their parents
before that—all of them silently kvetching, kibitzing
groaning, singing, all the way
back.

A Familiar Train of Religious Observances

My grandfathers and grandmothers board
in separate cars. The men hold on
to the leather straps, rocking and mumbling,
heads slightly bowed. The women swim the air
three times with their bent arms,
gathering it toward themselves,
then cover their closed eyes
with their palms. Eventually, they get off,
one by one, and disappear into the ether.

My parents, in retirement leisure, board
together. My father plays the sad clown
for the only little kids around, and both run
into his open arms. My mother offers her pruned
parchment cheek to an excessively dressed
and perfumed woman, then kisses her
in return—as if swallowing a stone.
Then everyone sits down.

In the reverie of motion,
my father murmurs syllables
he learned by rote as a child,
as did his father; my mother, not wanting
to be left out, moves her lips.
When it's almost time
to disembark, they stand up, arms
around each other—as never at home—
and around the strangers on each side,
swaying. Eventually, they disengage
and step off, one by one, disappearing
into the ether.

You and I, so busy Elsewhere, leap on
just as the doors are closing. We fumble
with the unfamiliar books. The train shakes,
and we lose our places. We rumble into stations
memorializing the names of our grandparents
and parents. It's as if our children
never were.

You bring along your father's
prayer shawl in its sueded bag
and I, my father's, in its velvet pouch—

as though, if you hood yourself
in that cream and blue, if I cloak myself
in that silver and white, we will each
be recognized and find arms
to run into, when, at separate times,
lonely, we disembark.

Inner Zest

Wearing her decorous "street dress"
with its collar of lace, my mother ordered only
lettuce and tomato on toast—dry,
a punishment of a sandwich—
at non-kosher American restaurants—
or the virtuous vegetable platter without butter.
She talked, mostly politely, to my father,
though she could never get him
to pull out her chair before she sat down.

At home she wore a "house dress,"
with tattered hem and a tear in the chest,
to cook and clean. She spat *Sha!*
The neighbors! in an exaggerated
whisper whenever my father
raised his voice.

At home, she ate sandwiches of thickly
buttered bread and radish, oily and pungent;
she ate jellied calves' feet
with garlic-rubbed toast—Jewish soul food,
humble, but relished with peasant abandon—
and she wasted not: sucking the juice
from chicken bones, gnawing them
to near-extinction, siphoning the luscious
marrow from the bone-chunk in the middle
of her lamb chop into her mouth.

But, suddenly diabetic, she more than followed
doctor's orders—stricter than the laws
of kashrut—with religious fervor,
both inside and outside, and grew thin
as a saint, mostly on vegetables—
dry once more—until she died.

Outside the house, as a kid, shivering,
I wolfed my first un-kosher
burger, rare and bloody,
and soon, I admit, coveted the taste
of all the discoverable forbidden fruits:
lobster and shrimp in spas of butter,
lamb seethed in a mother animal's yogurt,
ham crackling and clove-studded.

And now, on the scarce occasions
I enjoy them, outside or inside
(virtuous eating being much
more common), I flash on
and savor the salt of her:
not carving her carrot
with fork and knife,
but munching with unabashed, lip-smacking,
bone-crunching gusto.

Paid Work

With a wave like a flag's
over Yankee stadium, my young mother runs
down our Bronx street toward the subway
and her new job in a Manhattan doll
factory as I set out for school, apartment key
hanging from my neck on a red ribbon
she gave me, scuffing the shoes she polished
against the sidewalk. All day she will stuff
gray kapok into the cloth arms,
legs and torsos of pale pink baby dolls,
breathe in rag dust in the fluorescent-lit
perpetual dusk of the grime-windowed loft,
and yack with the "girls" over the clackety-hum
of the sewing machines until the boss squawks
about the output.

At lunch, she descends in the accordion-gated
open-sided lift into the blaze
of the honking Manhattan street
stampeded by busyness moving west and east—
boys running wheeled racks of tuxedos
and overcoats; secretaries and shoppers,
wearing veiled fascinators and feathered toques,
clicking by in sling-back sandals and two-tone
spectator pumps. A hurried pastry
and coffee at the counter of the luncheonette,
while the boss's bookkeeper wife—adorned
with her little heads and feet
of mink—dines on salami
and eggs at the deli, and mom is back
on the floor until time to rush
home again, and, when weary dad
arrives, gaily suggest dinner at the 161st Street
cafeteria for the three of us.

Sixty years on, I read in the *LA Times*
about Mukhta Mollah and Kanchi Hazi,
who skim like breezes over the rubbled streets
six days a week in their pristine shalwar kameezes,
on their way to eight hours sewing blouses
in the glare and din of Beauty Garments Private,
Limited, Dhaka, Bangladesh, and proudly send

half of their tiny salaries home
to their natal families—in villages
where mothers-in-law tyrannize
their younger sisters.

And I remember my mother,
in 1953, her eye aglint
with that fresh sense of entitlement.

My Mother, the Milkmaid, and Myself

My mother, though no connoisseur of art,
adored "The Milkmaid" by Vermeer.
She was an immigrant with little learning
"by the book" who'd lived in Lemberg
and Vienna—whether decently or poorly,
now I'll never know. I think she might have loved
the crusty pieces of stale bread—so real
she'd want to grab a hunk—about to be
a meal with milk. She often ate the parts
of food we'd never touch, like chicken feet,
so they'd not go to waste. She came to understand
true quality, but always hated ostentation.

Having waited ages to "fix up"
the Bronx apartment I grew up in—
for the brocade sofa and the silky coverlet—
she might have fondly noticed the kitchen wall,
that humble nail anticipating something
to hang on it, the maze of cracks.
She must have seen the broken pane
in the glowing window—sweet
as the once familiar and one's own.
I wonder if her eyes were pleased
by Vermeer's mastery of streaming light
illuminating half the sturdy milkmaid's face,
most of her starched white cap,
and the richest color in the room—
the royal blue, made from lapis lazuli
exactingly refined—used
for her radiant apron.

But mainly, I hope she saw what I now see:
the artist's reverence—for the maid of all
work's focused countenance, for her hands' embrace
of the unglazed jug and the simple act
of pouring, for how she watches the flow
of milk into the bowl with such majestic
calm. When my mother looked at
her reproduction of the painting
hanging over the credenza in our foyer,
I hope she knew—even without conscious
naming—that preparing wholesome
food, polishing my shoes for school,

and keeping our crowded apartment clean
had dignity. Because she already sensed,
and not without reason,
that the daughter in whom she'd
fiercely inculcated the value
of education had had too much
to value such devotions—and spoke with her
on sufferance.

Dream Displacements

Who sits with my long-departed father,
pillowed at the head of a holiday
table? The pillars of memory
waver in image-floating sleep. Am I
the favored child there in a living room
looking onto a New York fire escape above an alley
where the bone-and-rag man cries?—
the child in the bosom of her tribe,
upon whom the rays of familial love
pour and kindle?

Or is it my own far-flung daughter
I see in this dream, dipping bitter herbs
in salt water, under my mother's
melting eye—in California
where my parents long ago
followed their child?

Some essence fills these emptying
dream-rooms, a massed invisible
atmosphere, as if the departed
are a structure like dark matter
drawing the visible universe
together, and their descendants are still racing
to embrace ghosts, or to escape.
My children and I are children
bringing them report cards
for adulation; I am a child—waylaid
by an aunty in the elevator
as I return from ferrying kitchen rubbish
to the basement—who vanishes for cookies
and milk into the dim difference of another nest,
whose mother stands frantic
on the street corner, fists
clenched at her aproned waist,

until the distant past—so intimate—mists,
funnels, performs its disappearing act—
and I am liberated into the eternal
instant—

where the bereft dog who entered our bedroom
as you and I, love, lay down for our naps—
and settled her arthritic hips
like a low-rider operated by hydraulic
pumps—now raises her head,

where the two of us are late rickety nesters,
pillars in a household, a country
unto itself—this freestanding,
light-years removed,
faintly lonely cosmos.

Stemma

A day of bright winter haze.
I fold myself deeper
into my jacket and wrap my hands
around a cup of black coffee on my patio
table. After a while, I draw the cup toward
me, the liquid swaying like a boat
in double-time waves; the unpruned
wild, bare branches above me—
etched against a white sky,
mirrored in the coffee's
surface—seem to shake against the cold…
until they settle into a tracery
of naked arteries leading me back
to the souvenir pictures of my father's heart
angiograms with their little
"before" and "after" the-balloon-
pushed-through arrows—
from a time before "before"
and "after" were collapsed
into never.

When I take a sip
and set the cup down, it's as if
pebbles have been tossed
into a lake; cross-cutting
light breaks against itself,
and the image is obliterated.

This Country

My immigrant poppa, German-born,
was "a little roughed up" after Hitler
came to power, scared "once or twice"
by a knock on the door before he left
for America with his younger brother—
following his parents—in 1934.
Only his settled older sister
and her family stayed…
until they couldn't escape.

Maybe in order to live
in this new country, to have
a wife and child of his own,
my father kept his sister's story
mostly close within, his private
memorial flame. Maybe his heart
was burdened enough to break,
but he wouldn't let it
scar and harden against love—
unlike a few whom evil terrorized
beyond hope.

As a young child growing up,
here, in this country, I wasn't compelled
or even invited to dwell on, to picture,
the shattered hours of those relatives
I could never meet: the broken glass
on the streets, the stars shining
on their coats, the black engines
steaming in the station, the swallowing
fear in their stomachs, then the soup
of potato skins, the lice—
their starved flesh and protruding bones
becoming smoke about the time I was born
on a golden, free street.

But eleven people were exterminated in a synagogue
on Shabbas morning, here, in this country,
in Pittsburgh—native ground
of Gerald Stern, Michael Chabon,
Gertrude Stein—by someone who says
All these Jews need to die; and as I rage and mourn,
a sliver of imagination lacerates
my heart with fear, and I hear

the heavy boots on the stairs,
the rap of knuckles on the door,
and I see *my* aunt, *my* uncle,
my cousins—whom I've never seen,
who were folded away from me
by my father's love, who were herded
at gunpoint to their deaths—
rising out of the safely past and gone.

Selling

Heads thrown back after one
bubbly sip—the young in soft drink commercials
seem as lavishly happy
as lottery winners. They look
the way we imagine ourselves
on the stages of our dreams—glamorous,
anointed, spotlit—our luck about to spill
into graciousness.

And even in ads for walk-in bathtubs,
incontinence pull-ups, stair chairs,
dementia care, the actors don't merely grin
and bear it, but almost chortle,
like Cheshire cats who just
swallowed these amazing canaries,
though the old they represent
are more like expiring birds.

But the worst soft pitch: these "personal" Christmas
pictures I'm looking at again, taken
years ago in the dementia wing
of my father's "retirement home."
In another life, his face would say
This is ridiculous, even if he played along,
sat in the appointed armchair
by the tree, and hugged the enormous white
teddy bear prop, as instructed.
But he is in this current life
and guilelessly presses his warm cheek
against the bear's fuzzy one
and stabilizes the bear's plump feet
with his free hand, as if they were a child's.

Tiny Apartment Early Girlhood Recall

Our three rooms were once
the still center of the snug
world—like the earth
in the pre-Copernican universe,
around which the immutable sun,
planets, and stars whirred
on celestial spheres nested
like matryoshkas.

Summer mornings, I lay late, regal
in my bed, suspended stories
from the grimy city streets, watching stripes
of sunlight flush and vanish on the wall,
hearing the music of the blinds
Mother had tilted open while I slept,
as they swung out from the window—
cracked for the breeze's cool burst—
and clattered back.

Winter afternoons, stiff-wrapped
in coat, hat, boots, scarf, mittens,
lint on my collar lifted away by Mother's
spit-licked fingertip, I ventured out with her
to the eternal village—grocer, cobbler,
tailor, butcher—counting the icy steps there
and back in groups of ten
like an incantation.

Always, then, on our return,
suddenly unbearable coats
were shucked in the hall,
keys jingled into the figured
bowl, packages were dropped
with Mother's sigh of relief,
and our frozen cheeks, tingling,
thawed, in the steamy
hothouse heat—once the heavy door
of our apartment opened and shut.

On the Roof

The tar-like surface was warm and sticky,
as if it could be picked up and reshaped, and billowy
as the ocean on a mild day. When Mother,
carrying the basket of wet laundry, and I, the bag
of clothespins, emerged from the dim and narrow
stairs that led from the sixth floor
of our building to the roof, it took a moment
to get our sea legs. This was so long ago,
there were few TV aerials, and Mother wore
her tailored "street dress," as if leaving
our cramped and stale apartment
to go up and out was equivalent
to going "downstairs." I was still too small
to reach the clothesline, but I could hand her
the worn-smooth wooden clothespins
that looked like armless men with tiny featureless
round heads. She fought the weight
of wrung-out sheets and flopped them on the line,
where gradually she stretched them out
until they flapped like sails, white and brilliant
in the windy sun, all at once trying to fly
and staying in place.

From that roof, all city dwellers' unseen presences,
en masse, felt palpable to the far horizon.
The sky—washed and rinsed
with light, hung with thin drifts
of stratus—was enormous as the prairie's.

I think of other roofs I've seen
since then: the terrace roofs filled
with tanners' dye pits—indigo, poppy,
saffron—in Marrakesh, roof patios
in Damascus, on whose parapets
mint and oregano grew in small pots,
even the roofs of Cairo high-rises
where squatters sheltered in fragile lean-tos
shaded by fronds. And how all of us citizens
could breathe a little better in the higher, freer air,
and—perhaps more than the magnates
of my native city, surveying their infinity
pools and glamorous views
through penthouse windows—could feel the kinship
of existing under the immense
and common sky.

Saving the Dead

> *Our memory is the only help that is left to them.*
> —Theodor Adorno

We carry them inside us like persons
still unborn, as if everything they might be again
awaited them. The bodies of our mothers
before we were born: the once coquettish
bodies of our prim mothers—my mother balanced
on a honeymoon hayrick with my father,
his palm sweeping her face towards his
for a kiss, a white hibiscus flower blowing
in her black, black hair.

The bodies of our fathers, flat-bellied
in their crisp-pressed uniforms,
standing near the wings
of the Flying Fortress, on the deck
of the Massachusetts. My father grins
at a monkey on his lifted arm,
on a tiny island purpose-built
refueling stop. All those
kept safe for us by luck.

Time startled and lurching forward,
we still carry them:

The bodies of our mothers rocking
with ours, groaning with us
when we are ill—the smell,
still in my nose, of my mother's
richly metallic fertile blood
on the Kotex in the bathroom,
the carving out of her womb,
and so many others'—the decades
beating furiously away,
the long *a-a-h* of their sighs,
as they settle into our warm cars
to be taken to the doctor's.

The bodies of our fathers, their huge hands
under our backs as they teach us
how to float, their sturdy shoulders
we ride into the breakers—

my father's arms cradling
my four-year-old body zonked on
the cherries I stole from a tray
of Manhattans at an aunt's wedding,
home we go, home, on the subway—
the careless crowding generations,
the cracking of their chests,
their plaintive reedy cheeps, *But I enjoy it,*
when we urge them not to eat fast-food.

We carry them—their years fanned out
again, unshelved—as we are carried towards
the indignities of our own bodies;
we are together: undone by time/
about to be undone; undone/
about to be undone by the bodies
that carry us. And in me my authors dream
again, as I dream—imagining my progeny
re-birthing me in all my hope—
a lustrous dream of being carried
forward.

II

Late

I am musing, as we lie
in our bed before sleep—you, engrossed
in your book, me, wandering
from mine—after our day spent
tending the houseplants—
repotting the bromeliad and the orchid,
staking the leggy ficus…
I am asking myself what happens
when the days we lay looking up
into the canopy of breeze-blown
intertwined leaves in the bee buzz,
in the translucent green shade
shaking and flowing,
lifted and thrown,
are decades gone? What happens
when the world stops pulsing
like the butter-pat sun
dissolving into its own melt
over and over again, flashing
like a sped-up caution light,
when the squinted eye stops catching
its trail of gold coins slanting
down the sky? And then you vine the fingers
of your right hand with the fingers
of my left, something so quiet
and undesigned you never did
at night when we were young.

Short Dream of Old Terror

Last night it was my old unspoken love,
balding, a brass ring in his ear,
speaking through chipped teeth
of voyages and showing maps
of Rangoon, Poona, Mandalay.
He had a shop where he stocked
statuettes and rugs.
He beat the dust from one,
displayed it in the middle of the floor.
My heart ran around in circles
yelping *Sold! Sold!*
The doorbell tinkled
like the temple bells,
but he ignored the customers.
He wiped his hands.
He brewed a pot
of oil-flecked, fragrant tea,
then steered me to
a tiny curtained room—
only to show
where his ribs were cracked,
explain his heart's
fragility.

Brief Drift

A long walk to campus on a scorched,
quiet Sunday for a book I don't clearly need.
Not a soul on the street.
A collarless stray retraces
his steps for me, skids off again, slantwise,
for a pungent plant, neck stretched
for a low-flying bird.

Near the library lawn, a few people—
anchored as boats, benched
under trees—neither sowing
nor reaping. And all at once my bones recall
dedicated freedom: being eight or nine
and urged outside for hours after school
to guiltlessly loop and glide on my skates…

Easy right now to sit
on a bench—small talk nibbling
my line like a fish
I'll throw back, the carillon's quarter-hours
splashing my ears—
then, half-asleep, to watch the shadows
lengthen on the green,
the pages of the book open on my lap
riffled by the hot wind.

Non-Teaching Day

I drive by a long line of students
as they labor up the hill to campus
in the rare California rain—
holding umbrellas stiffly in front
of their chests, the way they'd hold
candles in a procession. They advance
singly, not talking, the steady tick
of the rain seeming to quiet them,
and turn their thoughts inward;
and each of them, alcoved in his private
space, achieving the hill's crest
where I stop at the light,
appears to me briefly dignified
as a figure in high relief,
with book or pen or pastoral staff,
on a cathedral porch. All day,
while I busy myself with my own rounds,
I will think of them flowing inward
and outward to the sound of bells,
their hearts so carefully
contained—like brimming bowls
of guarded water carried
from a desert well.

Wish

To skim, smooth-keeled—
ribs protecting my heart's cargo,
muscles sliding like oars
or wings—

my blitheness immaculate
as a child's skin;

and, within, my body's secrets unheeded
as breathing—

though the unseen bones
are like pumice, or sponges,
the skeleton holding up
the body's tent, collapsible
as pick-up sticks,
the sack of blood I am
quivers like a cut of liver,

though the inside will out,
the viny tendons in the hands,
the sharper skull in the face,
the mind, in its bind
of brain, will loosen and leak—

right now, in the azure air,
to hang glide
from myself.

Ageism

Crippled by arthritis,
but hanging on, she's all akimbo,
ears pinned back, eyes
riveted on me, legs stiff at obtuse
angles, like a possessed dog
in a horror movie. Or her feet splay
like novice ice-skaters', and her rear end
drips to the floor and she puddles into it,
settled for a moment as if she chose
resting, until she tries to rise,
nails scrabbling on the tile
like seismograph needles—a sound
I can barely stand.

She no longer bounds up,
hearing us rattle the leash
and keys, and walks
behind us on her walk, slow
as a felon on the way
to the chair. No more communing—
knee licks, soulful looks, racing
into the room I'm in—or cozying up
to guests, so they want to
take her home. Instead, she hangs out
in our bedroom, all alone, and drools
on the handmade rug that blooms
with moist discolored circles, like impetigo
that dries and re-forms.

I've wrapped her pain meds in butter,
cheddar, pricey pill pockets, hickory-smoke
flavor, but she gulps the package
and hides the spat-out pill for our later
find. Her housebreaking's broken:
she empties her bowels
in the breakfast room.
Was *this* relationship signed on
for better or worse? There are
times, touching her, I feel
repulsed—like those who never liked
dogs.

Namer and master, I contemplate
arranging over and out.

Or, I could begin to train
myself to love her in her brokenness—
as you and I, Pet,
must do with one another
before long.

Chronic This and That

Body that drags at me
like an enormous ridiculous
parade balloon that won't
float—goofy-nosed,
wide-eyed, useless—needing
all these handlers
to wrangle it, bouncing
and wobbling, stubbing
its stumpy toes, careening
into barriers, blocking out
huge swaths
of the horizon:

cut your strings,
lighten, rise, so I may
be (oh bodily comfort)
heedless
of body—not a boulder damming
the flowing stream,
a burr catching up
the mind, a seed
in the teeth.

Blurted Psalm, Night before Surgery

Dear No One: drape me,
reinless, over the backs
of these packhorse words
fear no…with me…
Let me be carried away.

Make me small enough
to crawl inside the caves
of these sounds and sleep.

My helpless tongue's
the flailing clapper
of my body's rocking
bell: Lull it.
Unhollow my heart.

Coming Up from Under, after Surgery for Multiple Fractures

At first, I'm pushing up against heavy, dark
water for what feels like far too many seconds,
though a few hours before I was dropped
into it, abruptly, as if it were luxurious
and soft as feathers into which to fall
and fall and fall without harm.
When I finally break through
to light—eyes fluttering and re-closing—
my body's weightless as a floater's
in the sea, shallow ripples of cool drowsiness
washing over it. In this moment,
no replay of gravity's knife-at-the-back
yank, of the shatter of bones
like ice in a bag crushed
by a mallet. Freed
of my broken self, I ride
my own calm swells
of breathing, as if, at a distance,
I am watching healing weave—
from the crumbled inside out,
from the ravaged edges in.

Couple Observed

> *Bodily decrepitude is wisdom.*
> —W. B. Yeats

In the hospital garage, he, bent,
limping, one hip higher
than the other, shining dome
of his head white-fringed,
lurches out of the elevator
in front of me, pushing
her wheelchair, and she,
haloed in white frizz,
slumps forward in the seat,
face turned to one side.
Then, astonishingly,
they stop, she brakes,
he helps her up, and, shuffling
in her bedroom slippers, back
stooped nearly ninety degrees,
she leans into the handlebars,
and, with preternatural slowness,
moves him towards the rows
of parked cars. And I imagine
the inequities in their histories
must be sleeping
in their graves.

We balance precariously
on the near side of the pointer
embodied/not; we could step off
our front porch into
the afterlife. But, if we are
lucky, we will reach
such equilibrium:
the dregs of bitterness
over two ambitious
lives unreconciled, of grief
for lost momentum
in the sun, all utterly expunged
by the violent equality
of age—the scythe before which
the whole field bows.

4 A.M., Suddenly Awake

and I'm on a tiny island
in a frigid, obsidian
sea with the beloved sleeper,
Hoar-Beard, beside me,
remote as his own ghost,
as if he's already sailed
to the unimaginable continent—
as one day he must,
unless I sail first.
Silence pings in my ears. I can taste
the ultimate aloneness like metal
on my tongue. I imagine grasping
a routine: put on slippers,
pull up sheets, fluff
the desolate pillows,
smooth the coverlet—like a kid holding on
to a blanket edge between knuckle
and thumb, milking it.
But next I hear the whistle
as the milk starts to steam and froth
for espresso, and it's morning, morning!
commonplace and miraculous
as the sleeper, awake
and hale, breezy in the kitchen
where we meet—as eggs for two popped
into the skillet like summer suns breaking free
of the sea's hold, bursting
into the sky, sizzling—
and the night an aberration
and a lie.

Banana Bread Bake

Best to use up those blackened
bananas on the edge of corruption,
the skin peeling off slimy mush
no-one will touch. *And so from hour*
to hour we ripe and ripe. And then…
I think of my Renaissance Lit
professor at Smith, quoting *As You Like It*
in our class of ripening girls, 1962.
Handsome, war-wounded (some said his leg
was wood), he stomped in theatrically
with his cane, then leaned down, slowly,
and stubbed out his cigarette
on the leg of his desk. Then he chalked
on the board the schema
that would help us pass all his tests:
a simple circle with *generatio*
and *corruptio* chasing each other
around the perimeter, and immortal *ars*—
worshiped by the New Criticism
all my English professors espoused—
slicing through on a vertical diameter,
escaping the fated cycle.

Oh modest *ars* of this moment!
I melt the butter in the microwave,
blend its unctuous gloss with the bright silk
of the beaten egg, diffuse the sugar within,
add and mash the nearly rotten fruit
that thickens the velvety texture.
Then I drop in drifts of flour—
combined with the baking soda
that will quicken the mixture and the pinch of salt
that will pique flavor—and stir. A mere
hour later, the tender, common loaf
is born, its sweetness suffusing my kitchen.
I plate a slice for my sole partner;
he looks at me with ripening,
undying eyes—Orlando, for this instant,
to my Rosalind.

Even Song

Outside for hours, stretching
to top the heavenly bamboo,
bending to cut the dry
lavender stalks, then taking
a slow stroll as the afternoon
begins to close: late glow
cherishing white garage doors, back-lit pine
turned into glass-beaded fringe,
the beads dazzling up and down
the needles until the drama
of the light quiets.

Thank you, I don't know
who.

And for lamplight's
bright halo beside
my reading chair,
over my bed; and for
my bed, the loft of its
covers. For sleep
when it comes, its loft,
its covering, I want to
praise, dear no one.
And to thank you,
of the blank signature,
for the ongoing book
I bring to bed, in whose world
I so easily remain—its pages
turning pleasantly over
and over like days.

III

Astonished Shoes

From the hospital window
the sky is a wistful blue,
and two purely pink contrails
looped lazily into it
begin to fuzz out.
The mild breeze
whips snow-pears on the balcony
into frothing bowls
of bloom, parachutes billowing
down to safe landing, billowing
down. While here,
in her stricken room—
where the jagged light jolts
as if a mirrored door
had just slammed shut—
when the therapist attempts
to stand her up,
my old friend pees
on his astonished shoes,
then crumples in a heap.

The Natural World

A full North moon glides up
behind my shoulders over the black lake
on which I dream I am rowing
whose shores are covered
in crusted snow—
like a radiant beneficence,
regal in beaten gold,
immense,
a powerful friend
who understands the comforts
of wordless closeness.

It silently swings
a censer of sheen,
flings purse after purse
of spangles and gleams.
My oars drip gold
as I raise them to rest;
the gunnels drop stars as the boat bobs
in the swells. How the liquid dark
spills awake, as if
warmed from within!

But my stark heart shivers
in my chest—even in this dream,
brooding on your frightening
diagnosis—and my cold hands ache
with helplessness.

    For DNK

How It Is, in Time

The thin skin of the arms
imprinted like sand
over which waves have drawn
back and back and come hissing in,
sweeping across each other, leaving
their echoes like netting.

And invisible beneath the skin,
the bones of translucent porcelain,
their lattices growing lacier, starker,
like branches in a winter forest
of birch.

And hair of hoarfrost feathers,
retinal smoke and mirrors,
spindle-ankle dizziness…
then something—a silvery harp
arpeggio, ice-sheathed twigs
tinkling in a mild wind—a prelude to
some memory but, after,
only an unblemished
Arctic whiteness, like music's
silence.

Scare-Crone

I know I'm going to look down
at my thumb tomorrow morning
and see a wen sprung up
like a mushroom overnight, the first step
of a goose-stepping cancer—
or at least that's how I'm thinking,
driving home from visiting my coeval friend
whose body's a clumpy puddle, a slumping
pudding, who, as we leave
for the restaurant, squashes
an ancient discolored cap over her white-stubbled head—
(she cannot care, that scares me so) around which
the black crows circle, cawing,
and who's so goddamned un-self-pitying.

I pity, I admire, growing fiercer
for music music music—not
to be stuck in the musty corner
at the living dance, drooping
wall-weed in ill-fitting frumpy skin.
I want to throw shots back
into my open mouth—let my delicate
stomach rebel—and throw up
all the virtues—acceptance,
patience, dignity in decline.

I'm not going to stock pretty leak-control panties
or plan ahead for babbling on the heath,
though I can see my own crows
coming to roost—the crow of bone
crumble, the crow of dental
devastation, the crow of deranged feet.
But the black ox has not yet trod
definitively on my toe, and so—my luxury—
I hate the crows that get
in my face and try
to fend them off:
this one, feathers mangy with parasites,
who waddles near my right eye
wearing a groove; this one, twig-tool
held in his beak, who works his signature
trefoil by my left.
I shimmer my eyelids, wave
my hands, though their cousins

flock to my lips, as if digging the furrows
above and below will yield seeds,
though they land on my fingers,
my arms; though I'm on the train
to nightmare, though I'm on the train
to scare, I don my flowy clothes
and, shining like shook foil,
dance in my glitter and glow.

Now

I am happy to live in the ken
of canines, to be taken in
by their gaze, and to gaze
on them, for the long moments of saying
nothing. I like to wait out
the nano-delay—a bacon-bit in my palm
under a cartilaginous nose—
until a nostril quivers, and to imagine
all 300 million olfactory receptors sieving
the air. I love the warmth of mammalian
weight, gift-wrapped in fur, the soothe
to my fingers of flanks.
I would have dogs teach me how
to lie on the lawn with no purpose more
than the grass has—to breathe in the sun—
or to sit on the sofa, chin on the sill,
regarding the window all afternoon.

Now that my aching hip and knee
make me want to mewl at 3 a.m.,
now that so many friends I romped with
are fading or gone, if any joy comes,
I want it to spin me around so my feet
leave the ground; I want to grab
whatever treat the world throws
into my mouth, to chew it at once
and completely, without nostalgia,
without shame.

Definitional

Irresistible belly dance music on,
we girls, all alone—during my quick visit
from the opposite coast—shoulders wiggling,
hips twitching, spring
into crazy moves in my daughter's tiny
living room in our jeans and tees—
she, with the munged cartilage
excised from her right knee, leading;
I, with my tender knees,
one replaced, one not;
and my six-year-old granddaughter
of the shy sidelong smile,
the only one of us whole—all
go for it: undulate
and kick, furl
and unfurl hands, whirl
and dip and drop, laughing,
into chairs, trying to catch
our breaths. I have fed
on the good reliable bread
of contentment, but this
was dripping fistfuls of sequin confetti
flung into the air and hanging for a moment
crackling like fireworks—this sudden,
utterly impractical, small sweet
of joy.

Gold

Such rare visits, and usually on the third
day, my middle-aged son,
living a continent and an ocean away, says—
as if he's had a chance to ponder it,
and it's quite a pleasant surprise—
"It's really nice to see you,
Mom," and gives me a quick embrace,
like a light wool shawl stolen
from my shoulders just as I begin
to appreciate its warmth.
Which is notable, nevertheless,
because his greeting and good-bye hugs
always preserve the space between us
like a band of insulating air
and make me think of the way men
make even quicker work of mutual pats
on the back. But, this time—
he was in the kitchen,
rinsing dishes for the machine,
and I was ferrying the last ones
from the table, and everyone else was, I don't know,
blocked out by the shine, when he said
"It's really nice to see you, Mom, can I have
a hug?"—*praise memory's push-down storage
unerased, praise swift retrieval*—
and "Of course" (of course!) I said,
depositing my dishes on the counter with tempered
alacrity. "It feels good to hug you, Mom," he said
during the long seconds beaten out
like gold to blazing brilliance,
"And to hug you, too,"
thickly, I murmured.

My 8-Year-Old Granddaughter Discovers the Arbitrariness of the Sign

My daughter reports from afar
that my beloved girl, turned
philosopher—told to get into her teammate's mother's
car for soccer practice—said: "Why is a car
CAR?" Then louder, exasperated hands
clutched at her waist, "I mean
what is CAR?" Then, "What is a WORD?"
she apparently almost shouted,
before heading out (her mom saying, "Later!")—
as if she'd been fooled,
and was now getting wise to the ruse.

I remember being a kid saying
ANKLE ANKLE ANKLE a hundred
times over, until it dissolved into a sea
of non-meaning and couldn't be
recovered for a while—no boat
even making it out there with a search
party; only the tongue against the soft
palate *ANkle ANkle ANkle,* like a helpless
untrained oar slapping the water.
Scary and thrilling, too, like being unable
to move in a dark fun-house room
with tilting floor and walls—
all boundaries confused.

But my feisty girl was vexed!
I wish I was there to say: *the fun
beats out the frustration, pumpkin,
take heart.* If I phone and catch her this weekend
in the hour between dance class and soccer,
she'll probably have forgotten
her insight and sharing my own
will feel forced and stale, though I want to tell her,
*Wait'll you notice you're using phrases
arriving from nowhere, whose histories
are mysteries, whose meaning you can't
state. And yet they're redolent
as fresh bread and fit into conversational
slots neatly as bagels into bagel
slicers.* I want to share that my dad,
her great-grandpa, delighted in saying

"You're a gentleman and a scholar,"
whenever he won a few pennies
off a buddy at gin rummy.
And how I've spent smiling moments
anticipating dropping "And Bob's your uncle"
into the stew though I've no idea
what it literally means—or maybe just because.

*You're my referent for the sign GRANDDAUGHTER,
darling, though 3000 miles away.*

("And Bob's your uncle!"
I've written my part in a ghost
conversation.)

*Welcome to the world where solidities
are mostly space, sweetheart.*

Score a goal!

IV

Letter to the Ministry of Loneliness

> Britain makes loneliness a Cabinet-level concern.
> —*Los Angeles Times*

I take round trips on the Tube
during morning rush hour. I stand up
for maximum contact—for the warmth
and pressure of other bodies—
and inhale the steam
of coffee-and-cigarette breaths.

I offer to walk my busy neighbor's kids
to school. Their brittle voices ring
in the icy air, as if belonging
to another universe.

I try to strike up conversations
at the market where I buy
a single item daily, a bun
or tart. I stick to apolitical
topics: the BMW's windscreen smashed
by a flying cabbage, Saddam Hussein's
romantic novel.

Then I am home alone again.
I put on the kettle for a cuppa.
But the quiet is not lovely.
Nor the enclosure
of my own body. Everything's
supposed to be relative—
unless one's loneliness
is absolute.

City

> *the gift of loneliness*
> —E. B. White

The blur, the rush, at the hub of the expanding
universe, and then
the noise ground down to a purr—
the surround-cushion of it—at home
behind your own darkening window,
the you of you spurred like a flame
in your own anonymous cell
overlooking a recurrent screen
of windows: guarded, shaded, draped,
shuttered—sometimes limpid
as a smooth gray lake,
sometimes wearing the late sky
on their chests—or glowing,
but contained, or open,
yet purely black, or blank;
the dusk-blue isolation
your reward, the deep comfort
of all those unseen parallel cubicles;
and then of the electric hive
clicking on lights and TVs…
as if behind velvet ropes
in a museum: all of those close,
remote, fragmented,
cordoned-off scenes.

The Room

The window frames the crowns of distant trees,
white sky, roofs, a few wavering
branches of Japanese plum.

The scene floats,
a shining rectangle of light
on the double-paned glass
of the door, the blinds within closed.

A woman sits alone and still
in a print on the wall,
her gaze lowered, but not to the cup
whose handle her ungloved fingers wrap.

A woman loosely folds her glasses
on the desk across from the view.
Their framed lenses multiply phantoms
of themselves on blank paper under a lamp.

The window frames the crowns of trees, white sky.
The window's scene floats.
A woman sits alone and still, all lenses
seem opaque as mirrors.

Not Getting the Mail

Outside my window on the porch,
afternoon light blinks against
the stained brass of the mailbox lid
like a spider's web pressed
and released by the wind.
It is quiet on one frond
of the fern, which looks like something
singled out, something bespoke.

Nearby, in the patio,
a hummingbird flits
from crimson bougainvillea leaf
to crimson leaf, and the light
awakes again on the dulled brass.

I gaze in a stillness
that feels deep
as the one in which the letters
nestle in the dark,
in which they rest.

But I never stay.
My body busies
the calm porch,
lifts the lid—*now*
all's dispersed.

Distraction

Remember the silence of libraries,
of the great public reading rooms—
like snow falling and piling up indoors,
yet not cold—all patrons hushed and private,
the lamps of their minds turned on.

And remember lying in bed
with your book on the Saturday mornings
of childhood, passing through the mirror
or the secret door—no sound
but the faint rasp of your index finger and thumb
on the page's corner and the slight luff
of the turned page. How you looked up in surprise
at the windows' blaze of noon light.

Remember, on a summer porch, writing
a long letter to a distant friend—
by hand, in ink, on many sheets of tissue-thin
paper—a letter full of delicious news
you imagined her savoring as you wrote;
remember the spacious days framed
by waiting for her reply.

One day someone talks loudly on a new mobile phone
in a public square, and it's as if the fourth wall
of a house has crashed into the street,
yet the family inside blithely pursues
its strident, no longer secret life. Soon the talkers
gobble up the universal air.

Now there are chimes all day
inside your brambly, burry mind that branches
and branches and branches, though you yearn
for it to hold.

Now you dream of strolling, free,
through the empty streets of some imagined
hamlet in France or Spain, all the shutters closed
on a hot afternoon, your eyes lifted
for a scrawl of birds in the high sky,
the only sound the church bells pealing the hour—
it's so calm your ear traces
their almost imperceptible
trailing hum, until the air
gathers itself again.

Charm

My freshman year boyfriend—the slick dancer
from a lovely New England home, back in the double-standard
'60s—almost charmed the pants off my prim mother
and, I learned later, had been engaged
in the gang-rape of a townie girl.

Didn't Jeffrey Dahmer have charm? And Ted Bundy?

It's enough to make you put on tiger skins
and seek the desert.

Yet, sometimes I cannot feel my face until I don
my smiling interaction mask. Alone, in my blue room,
stewing in my own juices, I begin to dissolve,
then evaporate. I need the press of others
to make me condense, though my attempt
at charm, fashioned to interface, can feel
like an invader surrounded by leukocytes—utterly
resisted.

Still, talking on the phone this morning,
asking a favor of a friend, I felt my cheeks
chunk up with good will and my internal organs
all peacefully nestle. This afternoon, even my dog
put on the dog of good behavior—heeling properly,
as if trained—when my tiny visiting grandson
held his leash for his walk. And as I apply
my lip gloss and blush this evening
before going out, bizarrely I smile
at myself, trying to disarm my deep
doubt—charmer and charmed at once.

Bless us all—social beasts that we are.
We dish up smiles; we laugh in self-deprecation
as we flick cookie-crumbs from our lips;
we try to lift our blue-footed booby feet
in sync with a potential mate's, to lubricate
the wheels of social traffic with our luscious
dimples—as if we could soften the world
and shape it to our needs—our moon faces
beaming on our compatriots, dark sides
sweetly hidden.

v

Girl Brushing Her Hair in a Window

You round a highway
curve as you drive
through an unknown city,
on the way to somewhere
else, and glimpse in a window's dim
proscenium—curtain of shadow
behind it—the arm
raised, the sweep,
swathe of darker dark
re-collecting,

and know nothing
about her except
she'll never be
encountered

and are inspired
with such
tenderness—as if
your own
were a story
lost.

Here, We Are Gathered

Endlessness of ending
unbelieved, how can it be
in this plenitude of air, with the heat
of this latte in our hands,
this money in our hands, death,
yet not in the bones, in the breath,
until we sit blotched
and spotted, with our walkers
and canes, vainly adorning ourselves
in Curl Up & Dye? Until we sit,
pillow behind our bald heads,
toxicity in our veins—
death pressed against us
like a molester on the subway,
and we unable to move?

But no, not quite there,
not quite then,
for there is esprit de corps
in Shearly Beloved—where everyone's
hair starts out frizzled, or orange, or white,
and highlights, lowlights,
ombré, sombré drown out the fear;
and even in the infusion center,
there is quiet communion, comparing
of wigs and scarves, hope-woven threads
of connection that soothe, slightly,
during the set up of IVs,
the light closing of eyes,

until—
that pure knowledge incapable of sharing:
so this is what it—

Going Downhill

*He was really going downhill
these last few years,* outsiders often pronounce,
with hindsight, when friends or relatives flatline.
But, inside, by the cozy hearth of our own souls,
when we're wrapped in fleece, book in one hand,
whiskey in the other, to sit out
a bad cold—though we're born with dual citizenship
in the countries of the sick and hale—
home is always feeling well, and down
means coming up again—not death's greased
skids—until we're breathless,
bottomed out of hope in hospice.

How some of us guard against even a whisper
of helplessness! Like my always sturdy
spouse, who went down with a clatter
this morning in the shower,
thrown off balance while squatting to squeegee
the bottom of the glass door, and punched
a hole in the fiberglass wall, and bloodied
his knee, but got up painfully again,
saying *NoNoNo* to my outstretched hand.

My brother-in-law went downhill quite fast
this year, after his cancer was diagnosed,
as he tried to balance hope for more
with gratitude for his life, resignation
folded up in a back pocket.

A klutz with crap for knees,
I couldn't balance at all when, long ago,
he took our family on a first-time
skiing trip. The last of our group
to get on the lift (the bunny hill
closed, husband and kids somewhere
ahead), I fell rather than stepped off
at the top—into a drift. Shaken and cold,
bug-helpless on my back, legs twisted,
face hot, snow fluttering from a gray sky,
temperature dropping, the terrifying downhill
slope falling away abruptly below me—
that's when this kind man appeared,
assessed the scene, helped me

out of my skis and up, then
into them again, and never
once laughed. And I grasped
the ski poles he held out
behind his back as he schussed
straight down, gifting me
the ride of my life.

    In memory of DNK, 1945-2019

The Unasked Question

Hearing your soothing voice on the phone
the last week of your life, when you were in
home hospice, was like riding in the comfortable
family car to the darkness between stars.
How many of the dying would talk
as you did, even if they could talk?
If I am not in pain,
asking for obliteration,
I imagine I, like some, will weep
for my own consciousness, unable
to take in its extinction,
though the world has preexisted
our existences for busy millennia
and thrived without our kind
for billions of creative years—
all that vast time pristine as ice sheets
untouched by human being.

The cancer had come back, again,
and this time—well, perhaps
you'd had a lot of practice imagining;
perhaps you were utterly weary
in your skin.

But it was unchanged you, salt of the earth
you were easing towards, who celebrated
the cushion of family, the wise friend
riding along as hospice nurse, the delightful absence
of clergy, even pit stops with a little assist
and a lunch of pastrami on rye, though one
of your last. It was unchanged you,
weakening like a signal traveling on
past us, but still sending your extraordinary
frankness, your gift of lightening others
into comfort, whose words, heard
in my sadness before we severed the connection,
answered my unasked pressing question.
And the answer was: "You know,
dying is not so bad."

In memory of MFEB, 1927-2016

Voted America's Best Cemetery

　　—Sign on Freeway

Do most of the clientele
still like their views? Or enjoy
the Remember-the-Taste
-of-Coffee Klatch in the morning
whispery hour when the leaves all turn
silver in the breeze? Or the true Ether-
net, where all their posts still float?
Do they appreciate
the beneficial feng shui?
Do the new shades mention
the attractive stone benches where
friends may meditate
under convenient trees—if they keep
promises to return
after the obsequies?
Do the residents all praise
the quite long space of mortal time
before their graves are broken up
again? Or are there complaints?
About common-as-grass flat
markers, nose to the dust, chosen by relatives
chintzy to the end? About stand-up
headstones encrusted with tacky angels
or gaudy mausoleums—
bought by fat-cat family
just to flaunt their name?

No. Still, the dead abstain
from yea or nay—their ash eyes
blind, their ash hearts utterly burnt clean
of love of beauty, memory, hope,
and scorn.

Care

Who but the saints, who kissed
the feet of lepers and coolly looked
on carbuncles and ulcers,
can love the ancients moldering
in their beds, their wattles—
pale and grainy as plucked
chicken skin—trembling
as they moan?

When they were ghosts
of my far future, they were
papery and fluttery. They were
clean and removed. But now
so many friends decline—
the acute of mind wandering
and blubbering, the kind of heart
disheveled, rheumy-eyed,
not recognizing those
they blessed.

Will someone look at me
as I once looked at my mind-dimmed
father, his ever-growing bulbous
nose, his liver spots, his shreds
of charm made dearer?

Who will remember who
I am, or touch me
with an ungloved hand,
or even love me abstractly,
in my own descent?

Physical

First we own them,
skin and sinew, as if extended
from our limbs—whorls of new silk
on the warm scalp under our
soapy hands, oiled creases,
neat padded packages
in taped diapers
trundled into snap-up
sleepers, plump feet fitted
to our palms.

And they own
the willing us, giggling
fingers prodding our mouths,
then our cheeks squeezed,
our lips made fishy
by the flats of small
hands, our jaws pried open,
"to check for cavities,"
our hair "styled"—
straight up as I let my daughter
comb mine, making my scalp wince,
or straight out at the sides,
Einstein-fashion, as my benign
father, motionless as a model,
let me brush his.

And then the tangible years
evaporate, as they must,
and it's as if we've been
loosed, have drifted
into the dilating voids of space,
into an emptiness
where nothing ever touches,
our stories more and more
remote, impossible to access—
like the generation's before us—except
when memory flies us back,
quicker than light, to being Mom and Dad
or dreams our parents up.

Catch and Release

My fierce and anxious mother used to cast
an eagle-eye net over her only child and, later,
her grandkids—at the playground,
on the sidewalks—as if her gaze could corral
them like a sheepdog, because Something
was always crouching, like a lion in the shade,
to snatch the smallest drifter from the herd.

And now my own heart races outrageously
when any of my grandkids on their uncommon visits
can't be gathered into the seine net of my glance.
Like the littlest wriggler, all of five,
capricious as an unschooled fish—
the world his iridescent oyster shell,
to find and to admire—who loves to give
his folks the slip, and vanish.
Whom no one notices sliding away
till submerged to the neck in the calm, sliding sea
while the tide rises and the breeze comes up,
turning its pearly surface to shards.

Too late when I look up for the tenth time
from my book to scan the children digging in the sand
and shout his name *where is he where is he*
while his mother, panicked, runs
towards a commotion down the strand.

But oh! the nifty tricks of chance—
how a local fisherman anchored close in,
how he happened to look,
how he plucks you out,
as if in a children's storybook.
And here you are! our lamb,
our joy, cherubic
in your mother's tightening arms,
come back smiling—unaware—
from the world's great snare, uncaught.

And the Something, nearly fed,
slouches away,
unnamed.

The Comfort of Design

The great swell stretches wide
its maw in Hokusai's *Under the Wave
off Kanagawa*; its finger-like froth
hooks to whelm the boats
that ride in its trough,
and the shallow shells in which the oarsmen
double over themselves echo
but are dwarfed by the huge roar
of that monstrous concave.

Yet, the palate of the wave is striped
quite evenly in light and navy
blue, and the ragged fluffs of white foam
could be polka dots
on a bolt of rippling dark-dyed silk,
and the foreground white-caped
surge—that mirrors Mt. Fuji
in the distance—resembles a hill
of vanilla ice cream beginning to melt
in a deep bowl.

Imminent disaster flattens
with stressed edges and uniform
light. The terror of the monster wave
nearly subsides in the woodcut's designs,
"between the lines," as in childhood's
coloring books and tales—

where the dragon breathes out fire
in tendrils, and the trees and moss swallowing
the sleeper's castle are green symmetrical
dashes and dots, and the skin of the frog
the princess finds revolting
is as intricately patterned as her gown—

as if the world can tame
terror, death, catastrophe, hate,
and is made mainly for delight:

served up gratis
as a surprise cake, thrillingly
embellished with roses, shells,
stars, waves.

VI

Number and Weight

The number of stars in the universe may be 300 sextillion. Or perhaps only 100 sextillion. Subtract 200 incalculables. The mind yaws. Closes off. This is not like clinking change from the vending machine—sturdy quarters, slim dimes, chunky nickels. The multiplication table collapses, befuddled by zeros, spilling whatever was on it. O.K. Let's say the number of stars is equal to the number of cells in all the bodies on earth, as we've read somewhere or other. Is that more comfortable? Not really? Naturalized, but still uncanny. And on a small planet circling an average star in a middleweight galaxy only 100,000 light-years across, a group of blinded Kurds poisoned by Saddam's sarin lash themselves together and move into the wind. Merely a light-year's worth of pain? Who's counting? *Is* anyone counting? The Hutus arrive, singing and whistling, for the day's killing in the marshes where the Tutsis hide among the papyrus, drinking the muddy water tinged with blood when they can't stand their thirst. A Brazilian rubber company finishes off the Indian "parasites" in an Amazonian village by dropping dynamite from a plane; they return for the survivors, shoot off the head of a nursing baby, hang her upside down. The perfect children asphyxiated by Assad's chemical weapons lie neatly on the ground in their white shrouds, the foam wiped from their lips, their hair beautifully trimmed. Try to encompass history's pain in your mind for the mathematical challenge, or like some old god counting up suffering points for heaven. It boggles like the stars. Flood, cyclone, Stalin, Pol Pot, Kim Il Sung, Columbine, Aurora, Sandy Hook. Though a woman in a fitting room falls on her knees: *Thank you Jesus for this dress.* Hitler, Mao, earthquake, tsunami, Hiroshima, Vietnam, Mount Sinjar, the Bataclan. Though those Alzheimer's patients break out in song. The Crusades, plague, smallpox, Armenia, Biafra, Bosnia, Rwanda, Darfur, Iraq, Syria, Gaza, the displaced and slain to come.... The incandescently unimaginable sum? When one destroyed weightless soul is an entire world of lost light?

The Evening News

The sword, the axe, the gas, the drone,
the tanks, the guns, the IEDs, the stones;
the people, barefoot, bleeding, on the road,
so close to that wished-for coast, the drowned.

In dreams: tea poured three times
from a silver pot held high; the glinting
river or the sea by whose shores
mothers and fathers walked,
holding their children's hands.

Tell me the morning dew will bathe
every blade of grass, every tank
down by that river—and steel
will rust.

Tell me the doors of dawn
will open—and my scrolled-tight
heart unclench.

Tell me the child in the rubble
of the destroyed city
still breathes
and will be held aloft.

All-Purpose Elegy

Moon slid down the sky's face
and shattered, an icicle
broken-necked.

Night dipped in his pail
of shadows
and smothered the scattered
stars.

Then Void collapsed on itself
until it cried
out,

when Being raised her curved left palm
to her right
and closed the parenthesis
after your name.

The Watchers

Forbearant clouds—
frothy with ruffles
endlessly adjusted,

airy shoulders turning
and turning away
so slowly, no pose
resisted.

Or burgeoning into
clear air, or deep-veiled
and misted, or dispersed—
without protest.

Or, in the late afternoon,
floating like deserted
cities on a translucent,
cyan lake,
swallowing darkness
before the sky does
high above us—

who stride the shining earth
for this brief
startling moment.

Unfinished Painting

—Norham Castle, Sunrise, J. M. W. Turner

The lemony sun, freshly
juiced, in the air,
its mirror-glow—melting butter
in the shallow pan
of the lake. Earth, heavens,
waters, barely
divided.

A human construction on the right vaporized
to the vaguest taupe, the castle itself only blue
smoke thickening into a suggestion
of deeply indented cliffs.

Only one solidity, a cow splotched
with silky brown—the others on the shore
after her kind yet to materialize.
Head down, she laps water-earth-sky,
seeming to siphon off the possibility
of colors deepening, as if to keep
the sixth day of the world
from being complete.

Stillness

—Late afternoon, December, Southern California

As if an invisible bell
had been dropped
over the world. The leaves
of the willow stopped swaying
back and forth like a porch swing.
The feathery paloverde
stopped dusting the sky.
The long gold light
lay down. Shadows pooled
on lawns. Every rapt thing
paid the utmost attention,
waiting.

If ever I had been
that quiet, listening,
who knows
what I would have heard.

Terrestrial

Pale gibbous rock,
craters and mountains almost
showing, blooming
into the blue wash of early evening,
as I leave the grocery, looking up.
And the black birds
flowing underneath,
scrolling and unscrolling—

"What are you gazing at?" someone on her way in asks,
expectation in her voice,
as if a planetary phenomenon
might be occurring.

"Just the Moon," I say.
Our piece of stone, low
in the wide brush of sky,
claimable, familiar.
Strange. For a moment not
the Moon, silver disc
hammered to an adornment's
thinness, but simply a moon
in its 3D rockiness—
as if I were looking out
at a barren body, spun
off a spiraling exoplanet
over some primordial horizon.

Yet, how soon, unhesitating,
evening sinks down,
with slow, accustomed graciousness,
as I drive home. It's almost dark
as I carry my bread, cheese
and apples tenderly from the car.
The mica-flake moon fixed
above my chimney begins its glittering.

What an unearned sense
of completion as I unlock my door—
as if I'd been out for hours
in the perturbations of the air,
as if I'd helped steer the blazing sun
to its hiding place in the sea.

Acknowledgments

Grateful acknowledgment is made to the publications in which the following poems originally appeared, sometimes in earlier versions and occasionally with different titles:

Adanna: "The Room"
Avatar Review: "Chronic This and That," "Scare-Crone," "Terrestrial," "Wish"
Connotation Press: "Catch and Release," "Now"
The Ekphrastic Review: "Unfinished Painting"
Ghost Town: "Even Song"
Juniper: "Non-Teaching Day"
Life and Legends: "Astonished Shoes," "Paid Work"
Light: "Short Dream of Old Terror"
Loch Raven Review: "Banana Bread Bake" (published as "Pandemic Banana Bread"), "My Mother, the Milkmaid, and Myself"
New Verse News: "This Country"
North of Oxford: "The Natural World," "Number and Weight"
New Ohio Review: "Selling"
Offcourse: "Couple Observed," "Dream Displacements," "Gold," "My 8-Year-Old Granddaughter Discovers the Arbitrariness of the Sign," "Voted America's Best Cemetery"
One (Jacar Press): "How It Is, in Time"
Peacock Journal: "Blurted Psalm, Night before Surgery," "Not Getting the Mail"
Poetica Magazine: "Musical Surprise"
Prompt and Circumstance: "Stemma"
Rattle: "Letter to the Ministry of Loneliness"
Redheaded Stepchild: "Girl Brushing Her Hair in a Window"
Slant: "Tiny Apartment Early Girlhood Recall"
Schuylkill Valley Journal: "Care," "The Comfort of Design," "Definitional," "Going Downhill," "Here, We Are Gathered," "Physical"
Sheila-Na-Gig: "Coming Up from Under, after Surgery for Multiple Fractures" (published as "Coming Up from Under, after Surgery for Multiple Breaks"), "Distraction" (published as "Once Unruffled"), "Inner Zest," "Saving the Dead," "Stillness," "The Unasked Question," "The Watchers"
South Florida Poetry Journal: "Brief Drift," "Late"
SWWIM: "City"
Tipton Poetry Journal: "4 A.M., Suddenly Awake," "Ageism"
Verdad: "On the Roof"
Verse: "All-Purpose Elegy"
Verse Virtual: "Charm," "The Evening News," "A Familiar Train of Religious Observances"

"The News," which is incorporated into "The Evening News," as it appears here, was originally published in the anthology *Spectrum: 140 SoCal Poets* (Spectrum Publishing, 2015).

My warm thanks to Christopher Buckley who read and perceptively commented on this book in an early manuscript, and to the members of my poetry group (Lavina Blossom, Charlotte Davidson, Elizabeth Morrison-Banks and Cati Porter) who keep the conversation about poetry alive and well, and whose responses have helped me improve a number of these poems. As ever, my deep appreciation to David Kronenfeld, for his abiding confidence in my efforts and steadfast support.

About FutureCycle Press

FutureCycle Press is dedicated to publishing lasting English-language poetry in both print-on-demand and Kindle formats. Founded in 2007 by long-time independent editor/publishers and partners Diane Kistner and Robert S. King, the press was incorporated as a nonprofit in 2012. A number of our editors are distinguished poets and writers in their own right, and we have been actively involved in the small press movement going back to the early seventies.

Each year, we award the FutureCycle Poetry Book Prize and honorarium for the best original full-length volume of poetry we published that year. Introduced in 2013, proceeds from our Good Works projects are donated to charity. Our Selected Poems series highlights contemporary poets with a substantial body of work to their credit; with this series we strive to resurrect work that has had limited distribution and is now out of print.

We are dedicated to giving all of the authors we publish the care their work deserves, offering a catalog of the most diverse and distinguished work possible, and paying forward any earnings to fund more great books. All of our books are kept "alive" and available unless and until an author requests a title be taken out of print.

We've learned a few things about independent publishing over the years. We've also evolved a unique and resilient publishing model that allows us to focus mainly on vetting and preserving for posterity poetry collections of exceptional quality without becoming overwhelmed with bookkeeping and mailing, fundraising activities, or taxing editorial and production "bubbles." To find out more, come see us at futurecycle.org.

The FutureCycle Poetry Book Prize

All original, full-length poetry books published by FutureCycle Press in a given calendar year are considered for the annual FutureCycle Poetry Book Prize. This allows us to consider each submission on its own merits, outside of the context of a traditional contest. Too, the judges see the finished book, which will have benefitted from the beautiful book design and strong editorial gloss we are famous for.

The book ranked the best in judging is announced as the prize-winner in January of the subsequent year. There is no fixed monetary award; instead, the winning poet receives an honorarium of 20% of the total net royalties from all poetry books and chapbooks the press sold online in the year the winning book was published. The winner is also accorded the honor of being on the panel of judges for the next year's competition; all judges receive copies of the contending books to keep for their personal library.

Made in the USA
Monee, IL
16 February 2022